EMOTIONAL INTELLIGENCE: THE SIMPLE KEY TO A HAPPIER LIFE

Allow Your Life to Blossom to its True Potential. Learn to Understand Emotions, Avoid Empty Relationships and Develop Social Awareness

Table of Contents

Introduction 5
Chapter 1: What is Emotional Intelligence? 7
   Emotionally Intelligent Character Traits 10

Chapter 2: Emotional Intelligence in Daily Life 15
Chapter 3: Building Self-Awareness Skills 24
Chapter 4: Building Self-Management Skills 39
Chapter 5: Building Social Awareness Skills 50
Chapter 6: Building Relationship Management Skills 58
   Identifying and Analyzing a Relationship 59
   How to Practice Relationship Management 61
   How to Manage Different Types of Relationships 72
   Other Tips for Managing Relationships 75

Conclusion 81

Introduction

You have heard so much about emotional intelligence that your interest is piqued. Whether you are a top-management official at work or a stay-at-home mom, emotional intelligence is important in your life. I commend you for taking the steps to develop your emotional intelligence skills. By doing so, you will only improve your quality of life from how you feel about yourself to how you feel about others, and ultimately, how others feel about you.

The following chapters will discuss how you can develop your ability to master emotional intelligence and to see great improvements in your personal and professional life. The book is divided into 6 easy-to-read chapters that will give you insight into how to manage your emotional intelligence.

The first chapter will give a brief overview of what emotional intelligence is. Then the subsequent chapters will break down the tenets of emotional intelligence into more detail. Chapter 2 builds on Chapter 1 and explores what emotional intelligence looks like in your everyday life. From this chapter, we dive right into building skills that will help you improve your emotional intelligence. In Chapter 3, how to manage your emotions will be discussed, followed by how to improve your self-awareness in Chapter 4. Chapter 5 explains how to use social awareness and relationship management respectively.

At the end of every chapter, there will be a special section dedicated to giving you skills on how to develop each skill in order to become better at emotional intelligence. Also, please note that throughout the chapters, you will learn about Valerie who does not have an idea about emotional intelligence and her socially bankrupt life reflects it. Please do not be like Valerie!

Hopefully, by the end of this book, you will learn a lot from Valerie on what to do and what not to do in regards to emotional intelligence. At the end of the chapter, bullet points of the chapter topics and activities you can do to help develop your emotional intelligence will be given. Take small baby steps and do not be afraid to feel awkward as you try to implement the changes associated with emotional intelligence into your life. Every journey must start with one step and it is difficult before it gets easier. By the time you finish, you will notice how much your life has improved just because you decided to take the step to be more emotionally intelligent.

There are plenty of books on this subject on the market, so thanks again for choosing this one! Every effort was made to ensure it is full of as much useful information as possible. Please enjoy!

Chapter 1: What is Emotional Intelligence?

Meet Valerie. Valerie is a typical American who is married with two kids, a house, and a white picket fence. Oh yeah, she has a beautiful black Labrador as well. Valerie would consider her to have an average level of emotional intelligence. She does ok at work. Her familial, personal, and professional relationships are so-so. She feels like she's walking through life. Not going fast or slow, but just regular shmegular. She doesn't always feel in control and sometimes has panic attacks because she is overwhelmed, stressed, and unhealthy. She figures everyone else is going through the same things so it is not a big problem.

Cut to one busy day where Valerie is rushing to work because she has not communicated to her family members that she needs help and all of the chores and housework falls on her. Not too mention, she had to stay late at work the night before because she is a people pleaser which made her oversleep in the first place. Picture Valerie in a car, speeding down the highway in the rain before she hydroplanes smack dab into an eighteen-wheeler. Her car spins out of control and Valerie finds herself pinned behind her steering wheel in her car that is sideways in a ditch. Of course, a Good Samaritan saw the incident and immediately called emergency services who rushed to the scene. After the paramedics help her out the car, she is whisked to the hospital.

The good news is, she was alive. The bad news is, she has amnesia and she has to learn everything all over again. Facts like her children's names, her husband's name, and her dog's name will be seemingly easy to learn. However, the nuances of emotional intelligence seemed much more difficult to learn. She has to learn how to identify her personal emotions, manage them when reacting to other people, as well as managing her social settings and relationships. Whew! Valerie is on a quest to relearn what emotional intelligence is, but Valerie is not alone. There are a lot of people who want to learn how to be emotionally intelligent and are on the same path as Valerie.

This book attempts to help people like Valerie and the readers navigate the tricky, topsy-turvy, abstract world of emotions and the unspoken rules that come with it. Unlike Valerie who is starting with a blank slate, most people have some type of experience with their emotions whether they have anger issues, are people pleasers, or are narcissists. Emotional intelligence draws upon your personal preferences and experiences to figure out how to survive in the world. In order to improve upon one's emotional intelligence, one must first understand what emotional intelligence is.

So what is emotional intelligence? Known in short as EI, emotional intelligence is the multi-faceted capacity of being in tune with your personal thoughts and emotions and being able to manage them in your daily living and in your dealings with other people. In order to be emotionally intelligent, you must first have mastery of who you are and know how to handle your emotions. Then you must know how to navigate relationships with other people, especially how to interpret and understand their emotions and how to be savvy in the way you respond to their emotions for optimal results. In other words, to be emotionally intelligent, you need to know what to say, when to say it, and how to say it. Sounds like a lot? You're right. Becoming emotionally intelligent can be overwhelming, but it is not impossible. It is a skill that can be learned with practice. Being emotionally intelligent is a trait many want to acquire because research has shown that emotionally intelligent people are deemed better leaders, better friends, and better family members. People with emotional intelligence do not necessarily have the highest IQ, but they understand how people work. As a result, their acumen in dealing with people helps them to be successful in a way that people who are not emotionally intelligent are not able to achieve.

Emotional intelligence was brought to the mainstream in 1995 by Daniel Goleman when he wrote the book *Emotional Intelligence: Why It Can Matter More Than IQ*. This book was seminal in changing how people thought about the power of emotions. Before this book, emotions were not seen as powerful tools to help you succeed. Emotions were seen as a hindrance. Goldman brought the importance of being emotionally intelligent to the forefront, but it was not an idea that originated with him. Way back in the day, over 2,000 years ago, Plato wrote that "All learning has an emotional base." Even though Plato had said that emotions were important centuries earlier, scientists did not always see it that way. However, in the 1920s, the idea that emotions were important re-emerged when Edward Thorndike named the ability to get along with others as "social intelligence."

In 1950, Abraham Maslow sparked the human potential movement and wrote about the importance of people enhancing their mental, physical, emotional, and spiritual strengths. From his research, lots of similar movements were launched and people began to build on his ideas. From this birth of new knowledge, two researchers, Peter Salovey and John "Jack" Mayer in the 1990s, have been credited with first using the term 'emotional intelligence.' In the article, Salovey and Mayer defined emotional intelligence as scientifically testable "intelligence." This work set the foundation for Daniel Goleman's book in 1995. From there, many different offshoots of emotional intelligence were developed. For the purpose of this book, we will focus on emotional intelligence as being composed of four different parts consisting of self-management, self-awareness, social awareness, and relationship management.

Self-awareness is being in tune with your emotions. If you are self-aware, you are great at identifying and deciphering your emotions and using them effectively when you react to a situation. Self-management is the act of managing your emotions and the reactions to any situation you may find yourself in. The word 'manage' is key in the definition of self-management. If you are great at self-management, it does not mean that you do not get angry or experience emotions at all. It means that you are adept at how you manage those emotions to get the outcome you want. Social awareness is being keen to the social environment around you. And relationship management is all about handling your relationships whether they be professional, personal, or even the relationship with yourself. In later chapters, each separate component will be delved into in greater detail.

To understand how one learns about emotional intelligence, a person must understand how our brains work. Our brain is divided into three separate parts — the basal ganglia, limbic system, and neocortex. The basal ganglia are at the root of our brain and it is considered the place where all our instincts reside. When you feel something in your gut, the information travels directly to this region of your brain without going through the other regions. This is information that you do not have to think about at all. The next part of the brain is the limbic system. The information processed by this part of your brain is considered to be processed on the subconscious level. Subconscious level information is a step above unconscious information and that information is right below our level of awareness. The subconscious level is where our emotions reside. It stores information about experiences good and bad that affect our behaviors, as well as it stores our value judgments. The neocortex is the next part of the brain. It controls your level of awareness. The information in this part of the brain is able to be accessed at will. It controls our reasoning, language, and thoughts. This brief overview of the brain is helpful to understand because certain activities suggested later on in the book target certain aspects of the brain. It is a cool tidbit to understand how the activities strengthen certain aspects of your brain so you can learn how to control your emotional intelligence better and be more aware.

Emotionally Intelligent Character Traits

How does someone who is emotionally intelligent act? People who are emotionally intelligent normally have a few characteristics that let others know they are emotionally intelligent individuals.

- Emotionally intelligent people have empathy. They are able to understand how others are feeling in any given situation. In other words, like the cliché says, emotionally intelligent people are able to walk in someone else's shoes. They are able to understand how someone with a sick child may be having a rough time or understand the importance of being nice to everyone whether they have experienced that situation or not.

- Emotional intelligent people also think deeply about their emotions and other people's emotions – a lot. They are pros at knowing how to relate and manipulate to other people in order to get the best outcome possible.

- Emotionally intelligent people do not run from criticism. They are able to take feedback easily without being defensive. They are able to take what people say about them, dissect the criticism, and take from the criticism what they may.
- Emotionally intelligent people are also genuine people. They seek authenticity in their relationships with other people and tend to see the best in people. Hence, they also are able to forgive and forget slights against them rather easily.
- People who are emotionally intelligent are very positive. They are not angels. However, they are effective at refocusing their thoughts, so they do not act impulsively and do something that they will regret later.
- Emotionally intelligent people do not run from confrontation. They face the criticism head-on and then go from there. They handle the conflict with ease, even if their egos are wounded in the process.
- Emotionally intelligent people are excellent communicators. They know their personality type and communication style and are able to effectively communicate with others and know the style in which they prefer to be communicated.

People who are not emotionally intelligent tend to be the exact opposite.

- They are easily flustered and easily angered.
- They are selfish and they only care about one person - themselves.
- They do not think before they speak and they talk all the time without any care to how other people may react to what they are saying.

- People who are not emotionally intelligent are usually not the easiest people to get along with.

Emotionally intelligent people are leagues ahead of people who are not emotionally intelligent. Interestingly, one can have characteristics of being emotionally intelligent and also have characteristics of not being emotionally intelligent. The key is to try and work on your emotional intelligence until you are competent in all four areas of being emotionally intelligent. This takes work.

For someone who has never ever thought about learning more about emotional intelligence, the information explained thus far may seem suspect. You may be one of the people who believe that emotional intelligence is a fluke. You may think that it is not necessary or important to be in tune with your emotions or in tune with the emotions of others in order to be a better person. You may think emotional intelligence is nothing but hippy-dippy foolery that has no place in the same sentence with rational thought. You may think that emotional intelligence has no effect on your success. However, think of that one person that you would not rather be around. This person always makes inappropriate jokes. They never know what to say. It is like they always have a foot in their mouth. These types of people have no self-awareness. No one wants to be around them. This is why emotional intelligence matters. There is no black-and-white version of emotional intelligence.

It is possible that you are good with some of the aspects of emotional intelligence and you need help controlling the other aspects. Perhaps you are good at knowing your feelings and you're able to manage your emotions, but you are terrible at communicating with others. Hence, your relationship management needs work. Perhaps you are excellent at navigating relations and social settings, whether they are professional or personal because you are great at putting on a front but your personal life is in shambles. You may need to work on your self-awareness. Or perhaps, you can easily be wonderful at managing other people's relationships. You can be the one friend that everyone comes to when they need help, but you are horrible at your own self-management. It happens. Just because you are okay with three out of the four aspects of emotional intelligence does not mean that you cannot improve the other aspects. Wanting to be aware of how emotional intelligence works is commendable and there are definitely skills and exercises that you can do to improve each and every aspect of your emotional intelligence core.

Yet, emotional intelligence can have a dark side. There are some people who are master manipulators. They are so good at emotional intelligence that they can draw upon what someone else is feeling in order to get the outcome that they want. These people know how to pit people against each other, play the victim, and play on people's emotions to remain in control at all times. If you are not emotionally intelligent, you can really fall victim to their traps rather quickly. One of the most important reasons for developing your emotional intelligence is to be a better person and to protect yourself against people who have nefarious intentions.

Lucky for Valerie, she is starting with a blank slate when learning how to develop her emotional intelligence. She does not have to be concerned about all the baggage that comes with learning a new skill. For her, she has to begin by learning what emotional intelligence is. So buckle up. The next chapter will go into more detail about how emotional intelligence affects our daily life whether we are aware of it or not.

Chapter Highlights

- Emotional intelligence was coined by Daniel Goleman in 1995 by his book *Emotional Intelligence: Why It Is More Important Than Your IQ*.
- Emotional Intelligence is composed of four different parts — self-management, self-awareness, social awareness, and relationship management.
- Our brain is composed of three regions that control our thoughts and emotions. By doing exercises to improve every aspect of our brain, one can improve their emotional intelligence.

Do the Work

- Why are you interested in learning more about emotional intelligence? Is it to improve personally or is it to improve in a professional setting or is it another reason? Knowing why you want to learn about emotional intelligence can help you when you get to a difficult spot in your learning.
- Do you think that you have more traits of being emotionally intelligent or more traits of not being emotionally intelligent?
- Emotional intelligence is composed of four different components — self-awareness, self-management, social awareness, and relationship management. Which component do you think you need to work on?
- Before emotional intelligence was brought to the forefront, there was a philosopher who said that "emotions are at the base of every decision?" Who was it?

Chapter 2: Emotional Intelligence in Daily Life

Remember Valerie? Yeah, things have not been going as smoothly for her ever since she's gotten home from the hospital. She has relearned basic traits such as eating and going to the restroom, but she has not discovered how to completely control her emotions yet. Her therapist keeps telling her that she needs to look into it, but she has no idea where to begin. The more she learned, she discovered that emotional intelligence is way more important in her life than she expected. Just like Valerie, emotional intelligence has a place in every person's life. However, she knows that she has a long road ahead of her.

Emotional intelligence helps our relationships with others. Emotional intelligence helps us be happier with ourselves and it helps people move throughout life a whole lot easier than if they didn't have emotional intelligence. Research has evolved to show that emotional intelligence has a place in every aspect of our life as well from the workplace to your mental and physical health to your family and social environment. While there are specific ways to improve one's emotional intelligence by focusing on the component of emotional intelligence that they are not as healthy in, there are a few general suggestions to help one improve their emotional intelligence.

One major suggestion is to expand the vocabulary that describes your emotions. When you say someone is happy, what version of happy are they? Are they ecstatic, mellow, or jumping with joy? When someone is mad, are they livid, disappointed, or upset? If you need help developing your emotional vocabulary, you can start by learning a new emotional word daily by going to the dictionary. You can even learn foreign words to help with your task. The more vocabulary you have to describe how you are feeling and how others are feeling helps your brain react to emotional situations better.

Emotional intelligence can be tricky because a person can hide the emotions that they are feeling. If you expect all people to cry when they are sad, a person who is sad and does not cry and laughs instead will throw you off guard. How about if a person is happy and cries for joy instead of smiling and laughing when they are happy? People who react to their emotions in a non-stereotypical way can cause you issues when trying to figure out how to react to their emotions. On the other hand, there are tons of people who are pros at hiding their true emotions. Someone can be boiling on the inside, but outwardly say that they are happy. If people are able to lie about how they feel or act in ways that always truly depict how they feel, how in the world are you able to determine the best response of responding to people?

Research points to a new way of understanding how our brain works which in turn will help us understand how to be better at being emotionally intelligent. We already know that our brain has three different parts that help determine your emotions and controls how to react to your emotions and the emotional responses of others. Researchers have now figured out that our brain works from an encyclopedia of experiences that we have. The more information we have in our brain's encyclopedia and the varied emotions we can draw from, the better reactions our brain can pull out from its encyclopedia of emotional responses in order to determine what is the best way to react to any given situation. (This is why understanding the different degrees of emotions by improving your emotional vocabulary are important.) Research has helped us to understand that even though people sometimes say one thing, their face gives away their true emotions. Maybe they are smiling but they have a slight scowl which points to their true displeasure. Maybe they are smiling but their eyes have sadness about them or their smile doesn't include their eyes. Understanding the nuances of emotions helps someone draw quickly and correctly from their brain's encyclopedia. This ability to break down emotions and their nuances are called emotional granularity. This is an important tool to have in your emotional intelligence toolkit.

Self-awareness is an important aspect of emotional intelligence in our day-to-day living. Since emotional intelligence is layered, this would be the first layer to master. Self-aware people are able to identify and understand their emotions quickly. A key benefit of being self-aware is knowing when you are engaging in toxic behavior or even engaging in overly happy behavior that can cause issues as well. When they are able to identify these emotions, then they are able to properly choose how to manage those emotions. For example, stress is a common issue that many people have to deal with. Research has shown that stress is a common denominator in certain chronic illness like heart diseases, high blood pressure, and obesity to name a few. However, emotionally intelligent people are able to deal with it easier and sustain themselves in stressful situations in a way that people who are not emotionally intelligent are unable to. For example, an emotionally intelligent person is able to quickly identify what stresses them out and then choose the proper response to that trigger. This is what self-management is. Knowing how to respond to any given situation and it is the second layer of emotional intelligence. When you are emotionally intelligent, you are able to properly de-escalate the situation when you are feeling stressed whether that is to alter your surroundings or properly handle your responses to other people. In some instances, stress is unavoidable especially if certain relationships you have bring on stress. Emotionally intelligent people find amazing ways to handle the stress to prevent a mental health breakdown. At times, a professional must be sought when dealing with stress and its impact on your life. That's totally ok. The key to being self-aware is the action part of the definition when you decide to do something about the emotions you are facing. (Remember, non-action is also a form of action.) Many people can identify issues they may have, but choose to do nothing about it or continue in the same destructive cycles. Self-aware people and those who practice self-management are able to manage the situation and come out stronger than before.

For Valerie, to improve her emotional intelligence, she has to rebuild her emotional encyclopedia so she has experiences to draw from. After the wreck, she spent lots of time at home recovering. She got to learn her family better and engaged with many health professionals that helped with her recovery. She also discovered Google which is an amazing tool that she has been using to develop her emotional intelligence. During this time, she was able to learn what types of things that made her happy and what made her upset. She noticed that having breakfast in bed delivered to her made her happy. She noticed that when her children did what she wanted them to do, that made her happy. On the other side, when the nurses made her take medicine she did not want, she did not like it. Initially, she realized that throwing a tantrum like a toddler did not help. She had to manage the emotion in a different way. She realized that she could express her displeasure in a different way. She could state that she did not like taking the medication, but would still take it. The key to remember from this example is that communication is the key when you are managing the emotions that you may have. Oftentimes, identifying the emotion is the easy part. The difficult part of being emotionally intelligent happens when you have to manage those emotions. And for many people, communication is especially difficult when you have to explain unpleasant things to people. However, emotionally intelligent person expressed how they feel and then take the action. Valerie realized that while she did not like taking her medicine, she would have to in order to get well. So the response she deemed appropriate to this situation was to express her displeasure while taking the medicine since it was necessary.

Social awareness is the next aspect of emotional intelligence that affects us in our day-to-day life. It is the third layer to master. The social setting in which you find yourself plays a role in how you handle yourself. You know the saying, "There's a time and place for everything?" It is true. Social awareness is summed up neatly in that saying. A person is going to act differently at home than they would at work versus how they would act in a religious setting or a social setting like a bar or club. To master social awareness, you have to pick up quickly on what type of setting you are in. Is it formal or more relaxed? Is it professional or is it casual? One way to figure that out if you have no idea is to look at what other people are doing. How are they dressed? Are they wearing skimpy clothes or suits and dresses? How are they talking? Are they talking loudly, normally, or are they being quiet? What kind of language are they using? Are they using profanity or are they using vernacular or academic language? To understand how to act properly, you can also look at how others are acting in the situation. Are they being loud? Or only a few people are being loud? Then notice how other people are reacting to them. Noticing how people act and how others react to their actions is a big clue on how to be socially aware. Are people who wear certain clothes acting a certain way or are they being outcasted? The key to mastering being socially aware is to become observant and notice what is going on around you. A trick that some people use no matter what social setting they are in is to be quiet, sit in a corner and watch what is going on. Socially aware people sometimes take people that they trust to the side to ask questions about social settings they may find themselves in. On the flip side, you have to be true in situations no matter what others are doing, even if it is deemed socially acceptable. For example, have you ever found yourself in a situation where it was ok to bully and make fun of other people? That's not a nice thing, but if you don't bully the other person, then people would be bullying you. Emotionally intelligent people are able to stand for their beliefs even when it is unfavorable.

Valerie had to quickly realize that social settings dictate her reactions. After taking the medicine she did not like, she has been approved to go back to her former job. She works as a customer service representative at a technology company that manufactures the latest software. Before she was involved in her accident, she was a top customer service rep. After going through a two-week training, her love for technology has come back. She is a pro at understanding the technology, but understanding how to deal with other people in a work setting is proving to be a challenge. First, Valerie has to deal with the customers. Next, she has to deal with her co-workers and then she has to deal with her managers and supervisors. She notices that the company is pretty relaxed. She does not have to dress up for work. Valerie is able to pick up on the playful banter amongst her co-workers and managers that make her feel more relaxed. The company also plays music in the background to help deal with the stress.

Everything was going well until Valerie has to deal with a very angry customer on a call. Flabbergasted, she is immediately quiet. She notices that the person right beside her seems to be on a stressful call and they are biting the top of their pen vigorously. Valerie has no idea how to respond. Her initial thought is to yell at the customer and hang up, but last week, she saw someone do that and that co-worker lost their job. The longer she waits on how to respond to the customer, she notices that the person's voice continues to rise. Valerie feels her heartbeat racing and she knows that getting yelled at is a stress trigger of hers. She looks around and notices that her co-worker begins to smile and talk with their difficult customer so she thinks she will try that. Valerie begins to smile and notices immediately that her heartbeat slows down. She talks slowly and begins to give the customer options on how to resolve the conflict. She notices that her co-workers are doing similar techniques. She begins to relax and the customer decides that she would like to speak with a manager. Valerie immediately transfers the call to a manager. Valerie was able to handle her social setting by observing what others were doing and making notes of examples of what she had seen before. In this came, the old adage "When in Rome, do as the Romans do" saved her. After that one incident, Valerie was able to continue being relaxed, yet professional in her work setting.

Relationship management is the last key component that we have to deal with in our daily life and it is the last component of emotional intelligence. Relationships are everywhere! Our relationship with our self is of utmost importance, but our relationships with others are just as important. Emotionally intelligent people know how to react to a situation based on the relationship they have with someone. A relationship with a homeless stranger on the street will be different from your spouse versus the relationship with your teenager or toddler. Knowing the dynamics of every relationship is very important. Most people have a baseline of respect and kindness for everyone they meet. This could also be described as common courtesy. But emotionally intelligent people understand the nuances of relationships, and when necessary, they can manipulate a relationship to get the results that they want. In this case, manipulation is not being defined as a negative, but as an action that emotionally intelligent people know how to use to navigate situations in their daily life. People who use manipulation to control people for nefarious gains are different from people who use manipulation to get the results that they want. Evil manipulators tend to cause destruction in their relationships, whereas, emotionally intelligent people are able to maintain their relationships and they are able to return the favor of scratching others back when necessary.

An often understated, important aspect of being an emotionally intelligent being is the importance of knowing how to manage your time. Time-management is a crucial foundation that emotional intelligence rests on. Have you ever noticed how calm people who always have it together seem to be? They do not ever seem frazzled and their hair always seems to be done? Well, time management is a tool I'm sure they are using. Just like emotional intelligence, time management is a skill that can be learned. Later on in the book, we will take a look at how important time management is and work on an activity to evaluate your time management.

Our friend Valerie is noticing that there is a difference in the way that her co-workers treat her versus her husband and her children. One thing she has noticed is that they know how to manage their situation to get optimal results. As a working mom, she is having a difficult time managing her responsibilities at home. On one hand, she has to handle her responsibilities at her job and on the other hand, she has to handle her cooking, cleaning, and personal maintenance too. She feels like there is not enough time in the day. She feels like her mind is racing all the time and she is having small panic attacks. She has no idea what to do except to ask for help from the different relationships that she has.

Valerie first had a sit down with her husband to see if he wouldn't mind ordering take out or preparing food for the kids once or twice a week to see if she could get some me time. Because Valerie quickly realized that the best time to ask her husband about something is after she serves him her famous lemon meringue pie, she asked him right after he ate a piece. Of course, he happily agreed. The next task she knew she needed to accomplish was to get her children, a teenager and toddler, to take more responsibility in the household. Instead of whining to her children, she knew the dynamics of the relationship and she was able to use humor to address the issue. Her children happily agreed. The stress from trying to do everything herself had begun to pack on the pounds. So she began to meditate, exercise, communicate better, and clear out her schedule. Valerie realized that reaching out to the relationships that she had and communicating her feelings and how they can make the best out of the relationship was important. Valerie felt super accomplished!

Things were going well for a week until everything went back to the way they were. Valerie no longer had time to exercise or relax. She went back to scrambling to do everything. One night, she hears a ring at the doorbell. It is Patty, the interim replacement to her neighborhood association who wanted to know when Valerie could take her position back. Valerie has a tumble of emotions and she is not sure how to react so she told Patty she would think about it.

As you can see, Valerie thought that she had everything figured out, but soon learned that the journey to emotional intelligence is never over. You are always learning and developing your emotional intelligence. Some days are better than others and some days are total, utter failures. Valerie's life feels quite chaotic again and she needs the tools of emotional intelligence to learn how to navigate. In order to do so, she must first learn how to be in touch with her emotions. She must learn how to thoroughly dissect what her emotions mean and that is the subject of the next chapter of the book.

Chapter Highlights

- Emotional granularity is paramount in helping you pick out a wide range of emotions to choose from. The wider your emotional vocabulary, whether the words come from foreign languages or your native language, the better you are able to create an encyclopedia in which your brain can draw from when trying to figure out what is the proper reaction to any situation.
- There are different tools you can use to prepare yourself with emotional intelligence such as meditation, exercise, and communication.
- Self-awareness, self-management, social awareness, and relationship all play a major role in our day-to-day life.

Do the Work

- Make a commitment to find words to describe emotional situations that you find yourself in. Try to pepper your

language with a few foreign words to give your emotional vocabulary and encyclopedia more nuance.
- How would you rate your level of communication on a scale of 1 to 10? Be honest with yourself.
- What are some initial thoughts you have on how you can improve your communication?
- How are you currently handling your time management? Is there anything you can get rid of?
- If you were Valerie, what would be your initial response when speaking with Patty? What do you think would be the best response for responding to Patty?

Chapter 3: Building Self-Awareness Skills

Valerie often has weird sensations. She has learned that these weird sensations are called emotions. She has developed a basic emotional intelligence encyclopedia to include words like happy, sad, flabbergasted, upset – you know the basics. Up until this point, she thinks that she is pretty ok despite being in a devastating accident. She notices that sometimes people see her and they tend to go in the opposite direction. She is normally loud. She's never heard of the word filter, so she just says what is on her mind. She also makes jokes that aren't funny and laughs hysterically at them not understanding that sometimes the things she says may be offensive in nature. She tries to be nice to people, but no one seems to want to be around her. She isn't sure why. That's when she has learned about being self-aware, the first component of self-awareness.

Self-awareness is the master key to unlocking emotional intelligence. Once you have a deeper understanding of what self-awareness is and go about becoming self-aware, the rest of the components of emotional intelligence becomes easier. Being self-aware is difficult. That's why lots of people avoid being self-aware. They delude themselves into thinking they are perfect because that's easier than facing the cold hard truth about themselves. Do not be like those people. I want to commend you, number one, for picking up this book, it shows that you are open to having an honest conversation with yourself. What should a conversation with yourself about being self-aware look like? What questions would you need to ask yourself? This chapter will help you have that conversation and start on the path of self-awareness. The first section is all about knowing yourself and the second is about how to motivate yourself to become the person you want to be.

Self-awareness is important, yet difficult because it is all about examining your actions. You have to look at your past behaviors and your present behavior to understand how you can change your actions. Self-awareness is also difficult because we tend to be biased about our actions. Let's face it. We think we are the greatest thing. Do not get me wrong. It is great to have self-esteem about who we are, but it is more important to be realistic about our opportunities for improvement in order to carve out the best life possible for ourselves. Being self-aware brings on a bevy of benefits. When you are self-aware, you are able to be more empathetic and compassionate to everyone that you meet instead of just being blinded by your ignorance and personal biases. Self-aware people are able to relate to a variety of people because they are open-minded and able to adjust their emotions to someone despite their own inherent biases and prejudices. Self-aware people do have biases, but they are able to identify those biases. Self-aware people are not blindsided by their prejudices to the point where they can't understand where the feeling they may have is coming from. Self-aware people know their strengths and weaknesses and are open-minded and fair. However, they do not get this way unless they have a heart-to-heart with themselves.

The first thing you need to do before you have this conversation is to set aside a day for yourself. Make sure that you will not be interrupted because this will be one of the most difficult conversations that you will have. You can bring tissue, pen, and paper. You can have your computer nearby if necessary to keep notes digitally. You can also buy a journal if you prefer to keep notes by hand without having to deal with individual pieces of paper. You can even have an empowering music playlist because you may need it. Give permission to yourself to feel every emotion that you may experience with no judgment then go ahead and buckle your proverbial seat-belt. There are no other people who can have this conversation with you.

The first topic of discussion you want to have with yourself is figuring out what personality type you are. There are lots of personality online assessments that are free, easy, and quick to take that gives you an insight about your personality. On the piece of paper, what are your initial thoughts of who you are? Are you hot-tempered? Are you level-headed and cool or are you a mixture of both? Whatever you are, think about it and then take an assessment test. One of the most popular personality tests is the Jung and Briggs Myers typology test or the Predictive Index. However, there are other ones that you can try out if you prefer.

After taking the test, you will next want to ask yourself a series of questions:

- Who is the person that you admire the most? What is it that you admire about them?
- What character traits do you love about yourself? This does not have to be related to emotional intelligence. It can be something that makes you feel great about yourself.
- What character traits do you love about others? What are those traits that you wish you had?
- What do you consider your core values to be? Think about these values from a spiritual, emotional, mental, physical, and financial perspective.
- Who is the person you want to be? Think about the legacy you want to leave. Who will people say that you were when you leave this world?
- What do you think your purpose in life is? For some people, this consists of who you want to help and how you want to help them. They take into account what activities they like to do and activities they do not like to do when making this decision.
- How would you rate your self-esteem on a scale of 1-10, with 10 being the highest?
- How are you working on your self-esteem? What daily habits are you forming to make sure that your self-esteem is high and you will not be susceptible to bad decisions?
- Are you working on becoming that person daily?
- What are your strengths? What things are easy for you and what things do other people say you are good at?
- What are your weaknesses? In other words, what are areas that you can improve upon? Weaknesses are also known as areas or opportunities.
- What daily habits are making your weaknesses worse?
- What daily habits are improving your strengths?
- How would your closest friends and family members describe you?
- Do people, especially your friends and family, typically tell you the truth or what you want to hear? Do they think you are

sensitive and tend to hedge how they tell you the truth? Or are they very blunt with you and are not afraid to hurt your feelings if you need to know the truth?
- On a scale of 1 to 10, how would you describe your communication skills? Why would you describe it that way? Give three examples.
- On a scale of 1 to 10, how do you describe your communication skills when you are angry, stressed, or arguing? Give three examples of why you feel that way.
- When do you typically analyze your successful day or successful days to see why they were successful? If you do not, come up with a time when you should start doing that.
- What do you do when you accomplish your goals or are happy? Does your celebratory behavior turn into negative habits?
- When do you typically analyze your horrible days and failures to see why it went wrong and what you can do to improve it?
- How often do you seek out constructive criticism that can help you improve? Who do you go to when you need to get constructive criticism? If you don't have anyone, who could you go to?
- What is your spiritual outlook in life? Go more into detail. What are your views about the afterlife?
- What do you feel when someone you know is successful? Are you generally happy for them or do you tend to get jealous? Think about the why behind your behavior. This will help you develop more trends.
- What do you feel when someone you know fails? Are you happy with glee? Do you feel like you are in a competition with them?

Once you go through all of these questions, a conversation you would like to have is with someone you trust. Ask them do they agree with the results of the personality test and with the answers to the above questions that you asked yourself. The trick is to ask someone who will be honest with you, yet tactful and constructive. You may be surprised that the way you value or think about yourself is not how other people look at you at all. Be sure to take what they say with a grain of salt because they have their bias as well. When you are listening to other people, do not get defensive. Be quiet. The only thing you should say to them is thank you. Combining your personality assessment results plus feedback from other people plus what your thoughts are will be able to get a clearer view if you are the person that you think you are.

The next conversation you need to have with yourself is to figure out what types of things make you upset. On your piece of paper, draw four lines to create 5 columns. At the top of the first column, write triggers. At the top of the second column, write reactions. At the top of the third column, write 'How Do I Feel?' At the top of the fourth column, write 'How Would I Like to React?' Then on the last column, write 'Steps I'm Taking.' Then brainstorm. What things push your buttons? Is it when somebody chews with their mouth open? Is it when someone pops their gum? Is it when someone tells you directions from the passenger seat? Whatever the trigger that upsets you, write it down on the left side.

Questions you can consider when thinking about your reactions:

- Do you blow up? Do you tend to yell and scream or say bad words?
- Do you just ignore what is bothering you until you blow up? Do you avoid expressing how you feel and find yourself blowing up before it's too late?
- Are you able to address the issue constructively? Are you able to be calm and solution-focused?
- How do you feel about your normal reaction?
- Do you think it is getting the job done or do you find yourself still frustrated?
- When you try to confront someone about the situation, are you doing it gracefully or are you being confrontational? Do you yell and scream or do you find that you are normally calm?

Now that you know what your trigger is and how you typically react, how would you like to react? Would you like to be more graceful? Would you like to ignore insignificant things that bother you? Once you add that, consider how you feel about these reactions. Do you think there is work you can do on your reactions? Do you feel like you are doing ok? Lastly, figure out a way to better manage your reactions by the expectations that you would. By knowing what your triggers are, you can better handle how you react to those things. This type of deep reflection is an important way for you to become more self-aware. It also helps you create a stress-management system to handle things that may stress you out. What are you going to do when you are stressed? Take the time to create that system now so you are effectively handling your stress.

If you've made it this far, great job! We have more introspecting to do, so go ahead and buckle your seatbelt. This is where things can get ugly. The nature of being self-aware is one of introspection and honesty even when it is uncomfortable. You have to take an intense look into your past in order to figure out where you're going in the future. So now we are going to take a deep look into your past.

The first thing you want to consider is what are the very best memories you have from your earliest memory to the present time? Then think about what are the very worst memories that you have from the earliest memory to the present time? Please take your time when writing these memories down and go in as much detail as possible. This is essentially a written record of who you are. Next, you need to think about the conclusions that you drew from those memories? What are the results and conclusions that you have from those memories of life? Do these conclusions help you make judgments about people or about life in general? For example, if you had a cousin that only kept tootsie rolls and threw all other lollipops out, does that affect why you only like tootsie rolls now? Do you think Tootsie Roll lollipops are horrible without ever having a Tootsie Roll lollipop yourself so you are unable to conclusively make a judgment about whether you like Tootsie Roll lollipops or not?

After you have your memories down and the conclusions you've gained from those memories, now you have to dig deeper. It is time to make two columns. Title this page 'My Beliefs.' At the top of the left column, write 'Healthy Beliefs.' At the top of the right column, write 'Limiting Beliefs.' Next review the list of conclusions from your memories and put the appropriate belief in the proper corresponding column. Which ones are healthy? Which ones are limiting you?

A limiting belief is a belief that is not necessarily true, but one that you believe based on experiences that have shaped your views. An example of a limiting belief would be that if you need to get healthy, but you see that no one in your family is healthy, you may believe that being healthy is not a big deal since no one in your family takes health seriously. Thus, you feel that being healthy is underrated and this limiting belief hinders you from seeking a healthier lifestyle. Limiting beliefs do not have to be just about negative beliefs. Sometimes limiting beliefs can be positive, but also hinder you. For example, lots of people have the limiting belief that 'The love of money is the root of all evil' which in turn causes them to have negative thoughts about money. They think if they make a lot of money, they will be evil so they do not seek out opportunities to make money which in turn would improve their life. Even though it is good advice that loving money too much can be evil, it is a limiting belief when taking it out of context and hindering one's growth.

As you examine your memories, ask yourself questions about these memories:

- Did we play a role in any of these memories? Do we need to take responsibility for any of these actions? Try to look at the situation objectively like you are a bird viewing the situation from a bird's eye point-of-view
- Can you fill any personal needs without destructive behavior? You can do everything in moderation. But are you doing anything in excess?
- Are you living for today or are you stuck in the past trying to fix any of these memories? Sometimes the past can weigh us down. It is good to see the past as a way to enlighten your future behaviors but not to the point of your past limiting your future happiness.
- Is there anything that you can improve to proactively handle any of these situations in the future? If you notice any negative

trends or cycles from your memories, how can you stop them and turn those negative cycles into positive cycles?
- Do I need to step out my comfort zone? Am I stuck in my ways? Do I need to eat at new restaurants, be around different people or travel some to open myself up to new experiences? When you go to the restaurant, do you order the same thing every single time? This one should be pretty easy to answer, but another big clue if people tell you that you are stuck in your ways.

While examining the conclusions you may have about your memories, you may also realize that you have some forgiving and forgetting to do. You may need to call someone and ask them for their forgiveness. No matter how big or small, make note of the trends you see in your conclusions and be honest with yourself about how these memories are affecting you now. Be mindful that if you need to speak to someone and they are not receptive of your experience, that's ok. Say what you need to say and move on. Try your hardest to make peace with the painful memories. In the midst of this activity, you may also realize that you need to set boundaries. Boundaries are important because they help you figure out how to handle people. If you know that certain people are not good, make a boundary to not be around them. If you know that during a certain time of the month, certain things piss you off more than other things, set yourself up for success and create the necessary hedges around you. At this point, if you notice you may want to talk to a therapist to do more work on these memories, do not hesitate to find one and set an appointment.

Doing this activity may stir up lots of emotions and that's okay. If at any point you need to take a step back, feel free to do so. Then come back. The most important thing to remember is that your emotions or feelings are important. They are how you feel about a particular situation. Be kind to yourself and be non-judgmental about these feelings.

This next section is all about how to become self-motivated and become the person you want to be. Self-aware people know who they are and the person they want to become. To start on this journey of being self-motivated, we have more work to do.

The next things we need to consider are your daily activities. Please keep track of your daily activities in your journal. You can print off an online schedule and fill it in if you need to. When you're filling in your schedule, make sure that you are tracking your energy levels, sleep patterns, and what you're eating as well. Questions you can ask would be:

- What time of day are you doing your best work? Think about when you are most productive. What other factors do you notice contribute to your productivity? Is it when you have peace and quiet and your kids are not around or is it when it is loud and chaos are around you. This is specific to your personality.
- Is this time consistent or does it change? Another great trend to notice when answering this question is to think about the moon. Are you most productive when it is a full moon or at another time?
- What time of the day are you not doing your best work? Knowing when you are not productive will help you to not schedule productive activities during that time. For some people who are morning owls, any time in the night does not work them. For others, the afternoons just do not work and other people prefer to be midnight owl.
- Is this time the same or does it change?
- What activities are draining you during the day? Do you exercise or hang out with exhausting people? Think of all the things that tend to deplete your energy levels.
- What activities are giving me energy? Do you notice if you have a certain schedule that it gives you energy? Do you notice that it helps when you are around other people who do not procrastinate? Make an exhaustive list.
- Do you notice any difference in your energy levels depending on the foods you eat? Do you have more energy when you only eat certain foods? Do caffeine and sugar cause you to crash

often? Does meat cause your stomach to hurt? Does eating a heavy lunch fuel you for the rest of the day?
- Are you getting enough sleep daily? For most people, 8 hours is recommended, but other can get ways with anything from 5-7 hours. When do you notice that you are most productive?
- Are you happy most days? Or are you miserable most days? How would you say that you feel generally? Do you feel that you are living in your purpose?

The next thing you want to consider is your daily habits that are building self-awareness? Are you meditating or journaling? If not, it is something you definitely want to consider whether you are doing these activities digitally with an app or with old-school methods like a journal, pen, and paper.

An easy template to use when reflecting on your days and helps you stay focused on being the person you want to be includes five simple questions:

- Did I learn anything to do? If so, what? Try to be as detailed as possible.
- Did anything go bad today? If so, what? Try to be as detailed as possible.
- What did I do nicely for myself today? Did you say kind words to yourself for doing a job well done or anything that would boost your self-esteem?
- What went great today? What things did you do really well today?
- Is there anything I can do to make tomorrow better than today? Be specific and list a way that you can make tomorrow better than today. If the day was a phenomenal day, you can write ways you can make the next day just as good as today.

You should also consider whether you should start meditating or journaling. To begin journaling, find a journal and just freely write about everything that bothers you. By doing the work of free writing, you are able to write about anything that's bothering you. You are in charge of your destiny. The great thing about journaling is that you have a record of your emotions. You can notice patterns and trends in your behavior to see what makes you anxious, depressed, or happy.

Meditation is another form of being self-aware. To meditate, find a nice cozy place that's yours and yours alone. Set aside a few minutes of your time every day to journal or to meditate. You want to practice breathing deeply from your diaphragm and let your thoughts gently go by. You will find that your mind and your body open up and will improve. Self-awareness is hard but necessary.

For Valerie, she thinks that she is getting the hang of what it means to be self-aware. She is becoming more aware of how others are perceiving her and has begun to try and develop a way to be more culturally sensitive. She has also laid off saying all the bad words that express her displeasure and the corny insensitive jokes. She has a limited past to work with that explains how she acts the way she acts. In her case, she is learning a lot of her behaviors from the television, especially reality TV, but she has come to the conclusion that the television is not how reality works. Thankfully, her husband and children have been patient with her throughout this entire ideal and have patiently worked with her to explain why certain things are appropriate for her to say and why other things are not ideal. She has been learning rapidly but still has lots of more learning to go. As she continues to be self-aware of her actions and how she carries herself, she notices that people want to come around her a lot more than they did before. Yet, she tends to have random bouts of not knowing how to handle the intensity of emotions that she is feeling. The next chapter will focus on how to manage our emotions now that we are more tuned with them.

<u>Chapter Highlights</u>

- Self-awareness is all about being in tune with your emotions. A major part of becoming self-aware is uncovering feelings from the past to determine how those feelings affect in the future. Once you do that, you are able to work on your self-esteem and figure out ways to handle your emotions.

- Asking questions about who you are and analyzing your past experiences can be a long process, but they are very helpful in helping you figure out how to be self-aware. This step helps you to figure out trends that are informing your current behavior and can provide insight on how to become the person that you want to be.
- When you are self-aware, you're able to live in the moment. Practices that help you be more aware include meditation and journaling about your experiences.

Do the Work

- What are some questions that you can ask yourself when you're being honest about yourself that was not mentioned?
- Who are some people that you do not admire? How can you avoid being like them?
- What practices are you going to incorporate into your life in order to become more self-aware?
- What time will you set aside to do the work of answering the questions about who you are and looking at your past experiences?

Here are some helpful scenarios that can help you with your self-awareness. This helps you to think through ways to be aware of your emotions and apply the concepts learned in this chapter. There is no right or wrong answer. You can take this practice to the next level by role-playing with friends.

1. You notice that every time you talk about someone to your spouse, they immediately began to act testy with you. You do not understand why since you are only complimenting the person and expressing how awesome the person is. How should you react?

    A. You should tell them to get over it. They do not have to act like a wet rug just because you give someone else a compliment. You are not in charge of their behavior.

B. You can ask them why they act like that every time you bring up this person's name. Give them your assumptions about why they act like that in order to break the ice.

C. You can bring the person over for dinner and then see if your spouse acts the same way in front of them. If they do, then ask them both to resolve whatever issues they may be having.

D. You can just avoid talking about the person around your spouse and keep your thoughts to yourself. If they are acting this way, this must mean that they are comfortable and you want to treat others the way you want to be treated.

2. There is a painful memory that you cannot seem to get over. You know that this memory is affecting your current behavior and you want to find a way to deal with it effectively. The person who is the source of this memory will be in town soon. How should you handle the situation?

A. You should write a letter and hand deliver it to the person. Then officially let the pain go once the letter is delivered. You can follow-up to see what their thoughts are about the letter.

B. You should invite them to dinner and explain the issue you have and try to seek a resolution. If they are not receptive to what you have to say, you can move forward without gaining any closure.

C. You should ask them to meet you at a boxing ring and fight it out. Sometimes letting your pain out physically is the best way.

D. You shouldn't say anything. You should reach out to a therapist and get them to help you figure the problem out.

3. There is someone who is constantly talking about your weight. You already know that you can stand to lose a few pounds, but every time you see this person, they remind you in a non-constructive way and it makes you uncomfortable. What is the best way to handle this situation?

   A. The next time they say something, sock them in the mouth. They need to learn a lesson, specifically how not to be so insensitive.

   B. Let them know that you do not like what they are doing. And if they keep doing it, then sock them in the face.

   C. Avoid this person. If this person comes around, give them the silent treatment so you do not have to deal with them. Do not ruin your mood to be around people you do not like. The feeling is probably mutual.

   D. Communicate with this person and let them know that what they are doing makes you uncomfortable and then request that they stop. If they do not, let them know that you will no longer seek to be around them.

4. You have discovered a limiting belief that you have. You are currently working on overcoming this limiting belief and have done quite well. However, you had a relapse and you are not sure if you can correct the behavior that your relapse has caused. What should you do?

   A. You should continue to work on overcoming this limiting belief. It took you a lifetime to develop this limiting belief so you shouldn't expect it to go away overnight.

   B. Mope and pout. If the damage is irreversible, just accept the damage and move forward. Having a pity party is sometimes the best, soul-cleansing solution.

C. Try to be proactive and correct the damage that has been caused. Then continue to work on overcoming your limiting belief.

D. Do not do anything. See how the cards may fall and then go from there. Sometimes we expect the worse and the situation is not as bad as we imagine it.

5. You have taken a personality test, but you do not agree with the results. You take another one and the results seem more accurate, how should you interpret the results?

   A. You should ignore them. These things aren't true at all. There is a certain percentage that it may not be true so do not feel bad.

   B. You should take another personality test and then see what it says before you make your conclusion. Two is better than one.

   C. You should take the tests results as the truth. Sometimes we behave in ways that we are not self-aware enough to recognize as the truth.

   D. Take the results with a grain of salt and ask someone you trust if they agree with the results or not.

Chapter 4: Building Self-Management Skills

Valerie has had great days and bad days. One trend she notices is that she never knows how to act when she experiences emotions. When she's happy, she tends to leap for joy, shout, and dance. When she's sad, she normally cries hysterically until someone asks her what is wrong. Then she can explain what is going on. When she's angry, she yells, screams, and breaks things. Everyone tends to cower and run away in fear. In other words, she typically goes with her base instincts and lets the card fall as they may. However, after studying emotional intelligence, she knows there has to be another way. After doing the work in chapter 3 to figure out her current emotions, without the ability to explore her past memories (thanks amnesia!), Valerie is ready to move forward with learning how to manage her emotions.

This chapter is all about looking into the emotional intelligence toolbox and pulling out the skill of self-management. Self-management is all about how you control your emotions after you recognize what those emotions are. Self-management is crucial in knowing when exactly to use the emotions that you have. Self-management is important to know that when dealing with a sensitive person to not to break them loudly or in front of a group of people. Self-management is knowing that having an attention tantrum in the middle of a store is not the appropriate time or place to handle your complaints. When you know how to manage yourself, you have tackled an important aspect of emotional intelligence. Each component of self-management works together to help you improve yourself management skill set. Self-management consists of four different components. They are consists of your initiative, having a positive outlook, a focus on your physical health and your emotional healing, and how you are able to breathe and relax.

The first key to improving your self-management is to fine-tune your outlook in life. Do you normally have a positive or negative outlook? You need to decide that you are going to be kind to yourself. If you usually beat yourself down, today is the day that you stop it. If you are one that generally has positive self-talk, we're going to take it up another level. Right now, make a decision that you are going to be kind to yourself and you're going to work on being the person that you want to be. Repeat after me 'I am a wonderful person and I am going to be the person that I want to be.' Because you have made a commitment to yourself, you have no choice but to accomplish. If you want to take this commitment to another level, you can even write yourself a special contract. Write a mission statement on the type of person you want to be, date it, and sign your name. You can also hang it up in a special place so you can look at it and know that you have made a commitment to yourself to be a better person than what you have been.

People who are emotionally intelligent usually are go-getters. So if you're not a go-getter, how do you become one? That's easy — you put in the work. You must first try to understand what the vision is for your life. Are you comfortable and secure in yourself? If not, you may want to try a few different exercises to help you figure out where you're going in life.

The first exercise is called 'Write Your Autobiography/ Obituary.' And it is just as the title states. When you go down in the history books, how do you want people to remember you? You can create this legacy by writing your autobiography or your obituary. Take a few seconds to write it down. There are many items that can be included.

- Where did you go to school? Where did you go for elementary, middle, secondary school or graduate school?
- What career did you pursue? Did you jump around in your professional life or did you stick to one profession?
- Do you feel like you were able to follow your life's passion? Did you feel like you were able to follow your life's calling?
- Who did you become? Did you receive any great accolades?
- What family did you leave behind? Were you married? Did you have any children?
- How would your enemies view you? How would your friends view you?
- How did you raise your children? Where they raised completely different than you or similarly?

- Did you have any pets?
- What do you consider your greatest legacy to be? It can be something you are famous for or something that you are not famous for.
- Would you be famous or make an impact on the people that you love?
- Where would you hold your funeral? Would it be in a church or elsewhere? What country or city would it be held in?

After you write it, take a silent moment and see if you're on track to fulfilling what you want to do. If you feel okay about the progress you've made so far, great! However, if you feel like you're unsettled and you are not accomplishing what you want to accomplish, that's also good. Now you have the opportunity to take the necessary steps to turn your life around and begin to live the life that you want to live. Being a go-getter is an important part of self-management and the only person in charge of changing your life is you. If you want to be emotionally intelligent, decide to live the life that you want to live. Do not find yourself living for someone else.

Another daily habit that will help you build self-awareness is if you are noticing and improving your self-talk. We talk to ourselves all the time. If we are saying positive things to ourselves, it makes a difference compared to when we are saying negative things. People who are highly emotionally intelligent use positive self-talk across to themselves. When the chips are down, they are speaking life to themselves. They are not using words like 'I can't,' 'I will not,' or 'I am not able to do that.' They use powerful words such as 'I will,' 'I can,' 'I am able to,' and 'I am going to.' Take a quick moment to think about your self-talk. When you speak to yourself, is it negative or positive?

Let's do a quick exercise to help you reset your self-talk if you need to work on that. It is time for your handy-dandy journal again. This time create three columns. At the top of the left column, write positive self-talk, in the middle column, write 'Negative Self-Talk,' and at the top of the right-hand column write 'Improved Self-Talk.' Next, reflect on the language you use when talking to yourself. Are you saying 'I can…,' 'I will…' or 'I will not…,' or 'I can't…'? What phrases are you repeating to yourself? Add them to the appropriate column. Then underline the action verb of those statements. Are the underlined verbs negative or positive? Now move to the right side of that line. Create a positive version or a more positive version of yourself talk. Then underline the words The Burbs twice in this section. If you are prone to negative self-talk, replace that negative talk with those double underlined words. Next, you'll want to change those negative affirmations to positive ones so that you are saying positive words to yourself.

You can take this activity up a notch by creating affirmations. Affirmations are short motivational statements that you can create. You can add this to your column of 'Improved Self-Talk.' Affirmations are mantras that you can chant or positive words that help you think and say positive things. Reflect back on your obituary. What is something that you want to do that you are currently not doing? Create a mantra and begin repeating it in order to get to where you need to get. Take out a sheet a paper or use one in your journal. Draw a line in the middle. On the left side of the paper, write the goals that you want to do. Then on the right-hand side, write a mantra that is directly related to that goal. For example, if you say I want to be a school teacher. On the right-hand side, write 'I will be a school teacher' or 'I am taking the necessary steps to be a school teacher.'

If you need a template, you can just use a positive affirmation in front of the goal and repeat that at least twice a day. The more you repeat it, the more the affirmation will lodge into your self-conscious and you will be able to make the right decisions that will help you reach your goals.

Other affirmations you can use include:

- I am worthy.
- I will succeed.
- I am able.
- I am loved.
- I am happy.

- I can do this.
- I am great and I'm working on my greatness every day.
- I am calm and at peace.
- I am self-aware.
- I am a beautiful work in progress.

To create your own affirmations, make the affirmation positive and in the present tense. You can create the affirmations to reflect your personal goals and habits.

The next exercise you want to do is a visualization activity where you visualize great things for your future. When you visualize, you want to be as specific as possible. If you want to be a teacher, make sure that you describe what type of teacher you want to be. What type of students are you going to teach? What does your classroom look like? The more detailed you are, the better your subconscious becomes rooted. As a reinforcement to this visualization exercise, you can even create a vision board. In a safe place, put up a board with cutouts and pictures that describe your goals and your needs. Look at that every day as a reminder of what you want to do. The more you feel secure in yourself and in your goals, the better your self-management of your own emotions will be because you have a grounded sense of who you are.

Another component of self-management is the health of your physical being. People think that being healthy has no bearing on your emotional intelligence, but it most definitely does. Are you as healthy as you need to be? Are you eating the way you need to be? Are you sleeping the way you need to be? If you want to be emotionally intelligent, you have to take care of your health. Oftentimes people take care of their emotional health but lack on their physical beings. How can you say you're going to be nice to people if you're cranky because you are tired? If you have a tendency to get angry, this can definitely affect your relationship management. Best believe, when you are upset, you will not be able to respond to people in the most constructive way possible. These are simple examples of how your health affects your emotional intelligence, but let's take this example further. What happens if you are overweight and you have chronic illnesses such as diabetes or asthma? You will definitely find yourself with challenges that people who are healthy will not have to run into. Not to say that people who are sick cannot be emotionally intelligent, because they can. The point I want to drive across is that physical health and physical well-being only makes your emotional intelligence stronger.

You remember the biography or obituary that you wrote earlier? How did you envision your life? Were you taking medication for the rest of your life or were you in pretty good health? Now is the time to act to your commitment to be physically healthy if you did not do that before. Now I know it is not easy if you have to switch gears in order to be physically healthy but it is necessary. Do you need to bring intermittent fasting or another type of diet that fits your lifestyle? Now is the time to do it.

The next key to self-management is overlooked just like your health, but it is nonetheless important. That is how you breathe. Breathing is often times called the life force and not without reason. Breathing is used to reduce anxiety in many people, thus a wonderful de-stressor. If you become a pro at breathing deeply and from your diaphragm, you are able to stay calm no matter what situation you find yourself in. To start practicing deeper breathing, you want to get comfortable and breathe in as deeply as you can for 10 to 15 seconds. You can repeat this exercise 2 or 3 times a day until you become used to deep breathing as second nature.

The next step to continue is to work through your painful memories. This step to becoming better at self- management is likely one that is going to be most painful. It builds on your memories from the previous chapter. This step includes continuing to heal yourself from past traumas. Anything that has happened to you in the past that is bogging you down will prevent you from being the best and most intelligent person you can become. Continue to work through those experiences. To represent your total peace, you can burn your journal once you finish. This is a representative of you moving on from childhood trauma. This will give you a burst of positive energy, a new outlook at your self-esteem, and a power to go forth in your new journey to become emotionally intelligent. If the trauma or memories of your childhood experiences are still very overwhelming for you at this point, you may want to consider seeking out help. Seeking help for an issue is not a sign of weakness — it is a very important aspect of healing. If you have insurance, you can check with your insurance provider to see if it will cover your therapy. Even if you do not have insurance, sometimes your workplace has a special hotline you can call if you contact your employer's human resources department. If you have limited resources and no insurance, you can then try to find a nonprofit to see if they offer any special form of therapy.

If you are caught up in the fact that you do not want people to know that you are going to therapy and it prevents you from seeking out help, you can look for a more private therapist. You can try online therapy which is a popular thing to do nowadays. There are even therapy apps. With a simple app, you have direct access to a therapist and you can talk to them without having anyone to see your face or know that you're going through therapy. The work that you can do with a therapist may prove more fruitful than the work that you do on your own. Yes, you can improve your mental intelligence without a therapist, but sometimes speaking to someone else that has no relation to you or understanding of your personal history can be very helpful when trying to work through your past.

In situations where you are faced with managing a difficult situation, you can try these few tips that will help you buy more time so you can cool down before having to make a difficult decision.

- There first is the trusty step of counting to 10 before you respond. Breathe deeply when you do. You can always take more than one to make sure that you feel calm before proceeding.
- The next step is to create a quick list. On one side, write your emotions and then reasons. Try to figure out why you feel a certain way. Scratch off what may be causing the issue and what may not be happening. Scratch off any reasons that aren't helping. And then what is left, you can see what you can do to improve the situation.

Valerie is exhausted from all the work that she has to do in order to manage her emotions. She feels more confined, but she has noticed that she feels better when people do not run away in fear from her or grimace when she is around. Valerie knows that she has a lot more work to do, but she feels very confident in the work that she has done so far. She will continue to work on managing her emotions and has even considered setting aside a time every day to continue to work on her self-management skills by breaking the tasks into small, manageable baby steps.

Once you get through the task of managing your emotions, the next step is to work on your social awareness.

Chapter Highlights

- Self-management is composed of four different components — physical health, emotional healing, positive initiatives and outlook on life, and relaxation and breathing exercises.
- There are a few exercises you can do to improve your self-management skills. You can make a copy of your obituary and make a commitment to be healthy. You can work on your self-talk skills, create affirmations, and perform visualization techniques.
- You can also get in the habit of practicing your breathing to help you improve yourself management skills when faced with difficult situations.

Do the Work

- Stress-management is also an important part of self-management. What ways have you come up with to handle your stress? Are you going to walk away when you are stressed? Visit your favorite spa, listen to your favorite song, or have your favorite meal? Will you exercise to take your mind off the stressful situation? Come up with three things to do when you are feeling stressed to help alleviate the stress you are feeling.

Here are some helpful scenarios that can help you with your self-management. This helps you to think through ways to manage your emotions and apply the concepts learned in this chapter. There is no right or wrong answer. You can take this practice to the next level by role-playing with friends.

1. Your co-worker begins to blame you for everything that is going wrong at work. You want to scream and shout that it is not your fault, however, you have been working on your self-management skills. What would be a great way to handle this situation?

    A. You take a deep breath and you calmly explain to the co-worker that it is not your fault. You also constructively advise them how to communicate with you. Playing the blame game is not an effective form of communication for you.
    B. You ask your coworker to refrain from speaking negatively and contact your boss. You let your boss handle it. This situation is above your pay grade.
    C. You fight fire with fire. Being calm has not worked. Being mean is the only way that your co-worker will understand that you mean business. If that doesn't work, you can get physical if they continue to provoke you.
    D. You bring in a third party instead of trying to handle it on your own. A third party will be able to speak to the co-worker in a way that you're unable to.

2. Every time you hear this one song it reminds you of a painful memory. What can you do to try to ease the memory from that song?

    A. Try to see a therapist and see if they can help you. Ask for recommendations from friends or search for a reliable therapist on Google.
    B. Journal and meditate about the personal experience and find some closure on your own. Also, be open to the

fact that some situations do not give you any type of closure.
   C. You can go to the people that hurt you, explain what is going on, and then forgive them. Then forget about the situation. Past is past and let it stay there.
   D. You can try not to avoid the situation and just think about it hoping but nothing can happen by not facing it.

3. Your friend wants advice on something but they are not going to like it. What is the best way to handle the situation?

   A. You can have a talk with your other friends to get them to tell this friend the truth so you do not have to do it.
   B. You can be honest and polite in a respectful tone. Then tell them what you really feel. If they could not handle it, then they should not have asked in the first place.
   C. If your friend is your friend, they will be able to handle your reaction no matter what it is.
   D. It is better to lie and keep the friendship than to tell the truth and lose the friendship. Sometimes the truth is not beneficial at all.

4. There is a person who constantly dismissed your feelings every time you try to explain how you feel. They obviously do not care and continue to do what pisses you off. You can't necessarily end the relationship, but you have to figure out the best way to handle your emotions in this situation. What should you do?

   A. You can give them a big cursing. They do not care anyway. After you do so, hopefully, they will not talk to you ever again.
   B. Avoid them. They are not worth wasting your time on to try and explain to them how you feel.
   C. Continue trying and talk to them. Hopefully, they will see the error of their ways and be nicer to you. If not, do not change who you are because of how they are acting towards you.

D. Still be nice to them and continue to express how you feel. By treating them the way you want to be treated, you hope that you can continue to kill them with kindness.

5. You have noticed that the affirmations you have been using are not working as efficiently as they were before. However, you've noticed that you have reached a block. You do not seem to be improving as much as before, but you do not see any drastic things in your life that suggest you are progressing backward. What should you do?

   A. You should create new affirmations and see how they work.
   B. You should create new affirmations and combine them with the other affirmations you are using.
   C. You should switch up your routine and try to throw in some visualization exercises and see if that helps.
   D. You do not need to change anything. Keep going at it the same way and you will continue to notice an improvement. Sometimes you have to have a breakthrough with what you are currently doing before you move forward.

Chapter 5: Building Social Awareness Skills

Valerie has done lots of good work on her self. She has improved drastically in the first two components of emotional intelligence that require work on yourself. However, she now has to combine this work on herself and figure out how to use it when she is with other people. For Valerie, every social setting that she goes to seems to operate differently. The people wear different clothing, they speak differently and she has to act a certain way in each setting according to the instructions from her husband. She's honestly quite confused. She wants to be the same way at all time but notices that most people shift who they are depending on their setting. Her husband had to explain to her that people are not changing who they are in different settings. They are only changing their behavior and doing what is deemed most appropriate. Valerie is now ready for the next challenge of figuring out how to manage her social setting and develop the awareness that comes along with it.

Like Valerie, once you are able to be self-aware and have self-management skills, it is time to layer in building on your social awareness. Social awareness can be difficult because people are complex. They are great at hiding their emotions by lying or not knowing what they want themselves. Because they are not self-aware, they have so much baggage that they are dealing with and project that baggage onto you. However, in order to be a fully rounded emotionally intelligent person, you must know how to interact with people as well.

There's a basic need for humans to feel connected to people. Other basic needs of human beings are to love, to feel loved, and to be valued and affirmed. That is necessary and it is an important part of being socially aware. We are socially aware you are also able to be empathetic and to put yourself in someone else's shoes. Emotionally intelligent people understand that sometimes you have your days and sometimes you have bad days. The flexibility to be able to go back and forth between these understanding is most important. The first part of being a socially aware person is to realize that there is good in every human. There is a tendency to only focus on the negative in people. However, when you know that there is inherently good in people, your reactions and interactions with them are going to be much more positive.

The next component of social awareness you need to develop is knowing how to give the right social signals and how to pick up on other people's social signals. You want to be approachable and friendly. The way to do that is to use certain non-verbal clues. You want to make eye contact with people and do not be afraid to touch them. However, you also have to be aware of how people are responding to your non-verbal clues. When you touch them, make sure that they do not flinch or give you any other key that they do not like it. If you decide to touch people, a simple shoulder touch or hand touch should suffice. You want to be mindful of people's personal boundaries and respect their preferences. Not everyone likes to be touched and that's okay. Another nonverbal clue to be mindful of is your face. Some people say they have a resting angry face. When you are in a social setting and you wonder why people are not approaching, think about your face and make sure you're not scaring people off by your unintentional facial expressions.

Additionally, how you stand is another important factor of being socially aware. If you are always hunched over, it doesn't demonstrate much confidence and people will not be attracted to you. The next thing you want to be able to pick up on your social awareness is if someone is being honest or being disingenuous. It is important to rely on your guts in social settings too. If you meet someone and do not feel comfortable around them, do not ignore that feeling. Do not feel like you have to try to make friends with someone if they do not feel that way. You can also observe people by what they tell you and their actions to see if they have integrity or not or if they are playing games.

The next component of being socially aware is to notice the social environment dynamics and fit in accordingly. This is called an organizational setting and the awareness is described as organizational awareness. In any organizational setting, you have to pick up on certain clues.

- Who is in charge? Who is everyone in the room referring to? Do you see any pictures around that give the level of hierarchy so you can quickly identify the head honcho?
- Who is not in charge? Who are the people in the room being completely ignored or being talked about behind their back? Is the person aware that no one likes them?
- What are the politics at play? Is it the person who is in charge or are they following the instructions of a larger force at hand? Is the person in charge there by nepotism or by their own merit?
- What is the emotional feel of the room and power relationships? Can you see that people are happy to be working with everyone? Does the room feel like its buzzing? Or does it feel depressed or all gloom and doom?
- Are most people generally excited to be there? Do the people look like they are joyful or are they dragging their feet, scowling and looking at you through squinted eyes?
- Are there smaller cliques within the larger organization? Do you notice certain groups of people always gathering around no matter what's going on?
- Are people dressed a certain way?
- What type of language are they using?
- Is the environment relaxed or formal? When people greet you, do they act like they are concerned who you are or do they look right through you?

Again, if you do not have a good feel for this, you can also ask someone that you trust.

Lastly, emotionally intelligent people have a heart to serve. This means that they put others first and are willing to be a servant or help others out. This does not mean that you are a pushover, but it does make people want to work with you. Others will be instantly drawn to you. From there you are able to learn how to be of service and keep solid relationships. So what does socially aware in this look like in life?

To apply and continue to develop these social awareness skills, here are a few skills that can help:

- Truly listen to what people have to say. You can repeat what they say in their own words. Notice how people react to what you're saying and how you're saying it.
- Observe people. People-watching is one of the quickest ways to blend in and quickly pick up on what's going on. You will be surprised by how much you can learn just by being silent.
- Watch your tone when speaking. Try to have a neutral, calm tone while speaking. Talk slowly, yet clearly. If you are soft-spoken, work on speaking in a voice that people can hear you so you do not come off as having low self-esteem.
- Have open-ended questions that you can ask people whenever necessary so you always have something to talk about if needed. You can Google brainteaser questions and pick out a few ready to use in emergency situations.
- Make eye contact with people. Look at them directly in the eye. Smile. If they look ways, try to turn back the intensity but still do not shy away from making eye contact.
- Say hello to people with their name. If you have trouble remembering names, try to give yourself clues of their names by making associations or alliterations with their body parts.
- Be empathetic. You do not have to agree with what people say or understand why they said it, just be nice about it. In other words, always be willing to walk in another person's shoes.
- Accept positive and negative feedback just the same. Say thank you and try not to defend yourself. Even negative feedback is important. The feedback may not be true, but what they are saying is beneficial because it causes you to have a better understanding of how people perceive you.
- Take ownership of your behavior. Always be willing to be the bigger person. This takes maturity and can be quite difficult initially, but it will definitely help you to move quickly through life.
- Avoid putting yourself in situations that you do not like so you are not uncomfortable. As you get older, you realize that you do not have to do things that make you uncomfortable. Yes,

you want to try new things to get out of your comfort zone. However, after being in social settings multiple times, if the vibe hasn't changed, don't feel the need to put you through future torture.

Know your strengths and weaknesses and lean on them when interacting with people so they can see the best in you. Another great way to improve your social awareness is to just have different experiences around different types of people. You can volunteer, travel, or visit a different part of town to observe more people. Just like building all the other components of your emotional intelligence, this is not going to happen overnight. Pace yourself.

Valerie feels like she is catching on how to change her behavior in different social settings while being true to herself. She has paid careful attention to the dress code and behaviors of different people in settings that she finds herself in. She is now ready to learn how to manage different relationships in her life and this will be the top of the next chapter – relationship management.

Chapter Highlights

- Social awareness is how you react to people and maneuver in a social setting. It builds on the skills of self-awareness and self-management.
- Organizational awareness is all about how you can pick out the dynamics of individuals and groups in an organizational setting. The quicker and most effective way you can do this will help you assimilate in different settings easily.
- Developing empathy and listening skills combined with having a service mindset are all great building blocks to improving your social awareness.

Do the Work

Here are some great scenarios for you to check out and role play. This helps you to think through ways to develop your social awareness skills and apply the concepts learned in this chapter. There is no right or wrong answer.

1. There is a person in the office who is picked on by your boss. You think other people are also bullying this person and it makes you uncomfortable, but you do not want to put your job in jeopardy. What should you do?

    A. You should ignore them and jump in on the bullying so you will not put your job at risk. This is what knowing the company culture and having social awareness is all about.
    B. You should tell the person to be encouraged and know that you have their back in secret. But in front of everyone else, continue to make fun of them.
    C. You need to report everyone to HR anonymously because your colleagues are not acting in a professional way.
    D. You should speak to the person in charge of your manager to let them know that what is going on. No one likes to feel left out. One only wants to come to work and not feel picked on.

2. There's someone who has told other people that they do not like you, but every time you see them, they are nice to you what should you do?

    A. You should go to the source and ask them if they like you or not. Do not shy away from the conflict. You may find out that they do not like you for reasons you had no idea about.
    B. You should tell them what you heard and get to the bottom of it one-on-one. It's easier for people to be vulnerable and feel less pressure when you are in a one-on-one setting.
    C. You should just ignore them and focus on your work in a group setting. If they have a problem with you, it's their issue, not yours. However, if they continue to push

you, say something so they know that you are not a pushover.
D. Do nothing. Their behavior does not affect your paycheck.

3. You really want to be nice to someone, but you do not want to come off socially awkward. What is the best way to meet new friends?

   A. You should hang around with people in the lunchroom and quietly listen and laugh. Then try to befriend people one-on-one.
   B. Let people know you are looking for friends and that anyone's interested should contact you.
   C. You should find someone who you think is nice by observing them and ask them if they would like to be your friend in a one-on-one setting.
   D. You should look for the nicest person you can find even though they may not be compatible with you, and ask them.

4. You notice that everyone is honking their horn at someone as they pass the street. You have no idea what they are doing. What should you do?

   A. You should honk your horn too. Other people are doing it.
   B. You should not honk your horn. You have no idea why the people are honking the horn and you do not want to do the wrong thing.
   C. You can ask someone on the side of the road why they are honking at this person. Maybe they can tell you.
   D. You should just keep driving and wave at the person instead of honking. That seems nicer to you.

5. You go to an event and notice that you are severely underdressed. You feel slightly uncomfortable. How should you handle the situation?

A. You should act normal. There is nothing wrong with not knowing the dress code. Your self-esteem should be so high that even if you were in a potato sack, you would feel comfortable.
B. You should make a mental note so you will not be underdressed the next time. Also, try to figure out why you had the wrong perception. Maybe you are not picking up on something in the social setting that is causing you to pick up on misinformation.
C. You should just go home. There is no need to feel uncomfortable. Besides, you can't keep ignoring people pointing and making fun of you all night.
D. You should stay and explain to people why you are underdressed. Hopefully, they will not make fun of you.

Chapter 6: Building Relationship Management Skills

At this point, Valerie has learned how to be self-aware, manage her emotions, and identify the social settings that she finds herself in. However, at this point, she has more obstacles to climb. That is to figure out how to manage the relationships in her life. There is the relationship with her spouse, children, and extended family that she must manage, then there is the relationship with her bosses and co-workers that she must manage as well. Just when she thought that she had enough to figure out, she has to figure out how to manage relationships with her friends too. She knew that there was some work to do. Since being self-aware taught her to know to be in touch with her feelings, she knew that she would have to think about the varying relationship in some type of capacity before she was to move forward and she was absolutely right. Relationship management builds on all three components of emotional intelligence and it is the last layer to master in order to be emotionally intelligent. Relationship management starts with being self-aware of your emotions and actions and then practicing self-management. Relationship management develops your social awareness muscle so you are able to manage the relationships in your life.

Relationships vary. They can be relationships with yourself or with others including family, professionally or romantically. Despite the varying nature of relationships in our lives, one of the most important steps in relationship management is to trust in people. Just like in the social awareness chapter, by seeing the good in people, you will be nicer in your interactions with them, even if the relationship was to ever hit a rocky patch. This chapter dives into how to manage various relationships in your life. Relationship management is a three-step process of identifying the nature of the relationship, analyzing the relationship, and then managing the relationship.

Identifying and Analyzing a Relationship

The first step you want to do in managing your relationships is to identify and then analyze the relationship. To start doing this, grab a piece of paper and then make two columns. On the left column, write down the important relationships in your life. In the right column, you will want to add your analysis of the relationship that answers these questions.

- What do you expect from the relationship? – Some relationships are surface level and others are more intimate. It is important to know what your expectations of the relationship are when you are analyzing the relationship so you will know how to manage the relationship. A word of caution. Not all people see the relationship the same way as you, so in order to make some relationships work, you can adjust your expectations based on what the other person expects from the relationship as well. Whatever they think about the relationship, you have to be willing to accept their perception.

- What you are contributing to the relationship? – Take an honest look and write what you are contributing to the relationship that is helping the relationship meet or fail your expectations for it. Are you doing your part? Or are you placing the blame entirely on the other party of the relationship? Use action-based words and be truthful.

- What is the other party or parties in the relationship contributing? – Relationships go two ways. Based on your expectations of the relationship, what is the other party contributing? Look at their actions and list them. Try to be objective, fair, and give them the benefit of the doubt. Are any of their behaviors in response to something that you did?

- Is the relationship meeting your standards or is it falling short of your standards? – Now is the moment of truth. Based on all the information that you have written thus far, would you say this relationship is successful? Is it meeting your expectations or not?

- Does the relationship make you happy or not? – Sometimes your relationship can meet an expectation but you are still not happy. This metric suggests that you look at the relationship and determine if you are happy or not. If you are happy, great. If you are not happy, is it because of your expectations, something you are doing, or something that the other party is doing? Be honest with yourself. You may be surprised. Whatever the answer is, embrace it. If you find an answer you are not expecting, do not try to deny it. Accept and then plan your next moves accordingly.

- What can you do to improve the relationship? – At this time, you may realize that there is lots of room for improvement in this relationship or the relationship is not salvageable. This metric is important because it focuses on what you can do to improve a relationship. If the other party does not want to improve, you may still have to end the relationship. By focusing on what you can do, you take out the variables that you cannot control.

- Is the relationship worth keeping or not? – You've done a lot of great analyzing, but here is the most important question. Should you keep moving forward with this relationship or not? Some relationships will be unable to get rid of either for familial or professional reasons. In that case, you have to figure out the best way to handle the relationship moving forward. Other relationships you have the option of letting go. If a relationship requires you to put much more time and energy into it that it is returning to your life, you have the option to end the relationship. If the relationship is only one-sided and most of the work falls on you, you may want to consider ending the relationship. However, if you deem a relationship is worth saving or keeping, do all that YOU can do to make the relationship thrive. That way you know that you have done all that you could no matter what the outcome is.

After doing this vital work, the next step is communicating with the other parties in the relationship. If a relationship is one that you want to keep in your life, you have to communicate your thoughts about the relations with the other party to see if they are willing to put the work into the relationship or not. This conversation may highlight that the other person does not value the relationship as much as you do or you may realize that you are on the same page and you both can move forward together. Depending on the relationship, you may not have to check in at all, since the relationship is never going away and the person has no desire to improve this relationship. In this case, you can just do what you can do to manage the relationship.

Even in relationships that are thriving, it is good to check in with the other parties every now and then. Checking in every now and then helps the relationship to stay alive. This allows any grievances to be aired out to make sure that the relationship is solid and everyone is happy. Now that you have determined what you think about relationships in your life, you have to transition towards managing the relationship.

How to Practice Relationship Management

Two important skills are necessary in order to practice relationship management. The first is communication and the next skill is conflict resolution. If you can master these two skills, then managing relationships will be a breeze.

To begin communicating properly, you have to quickly develop how to read what personality type someone is and how to communicate effectively with them. There are four different communication styles. They are the boss, the sensitive, the socializer, and the analyzer communication styles.

- The Boss Communication Style – The boss communication style loves to think big picture and leave the details to the little people. They are focused on actions and results. Being sensitive and patient can be a challenge for them, but they can be sensitive if they work on it. However, they can also be loud, demanding, and disrespectful.

Types of communicative phrases you may hear them say are: "It is my way or the highway."; "I'm right and you're wrong."; "You do not know what you are talking about. Listen to me." Their body language includes clenched fists, narrow eyes, and hard stares. They may also point their fingers. People can think of them as overbearing and mean. They can also think of them as leaders.

- o How to Best Communicate
    - Expect them to be direct and blunt. Do not take it personally. This is just how they communicate to get their point across.
    - Get to the point quickly and do not get off topic. If you take the conversation off course to other topics, they may get angry. Try to get the meeting over as quickly and efficiently as possible.
    - Before you talk with them, think about questions they may ask in advance so you will be prepared to answer their questions with confidence. If you waver, you may lose their respect or interest.
    - Be firm in what you have to say and do not let them bully you. If they see you are weak, they may overlook everything you have to say and it may be difficult to gain their respect or confidence.
- o What to Avoid When Communicating
    - Do not try to engage in small talk. They do not care. They may even ask you why you are

asking them. Keep your tone professional and to the point.

- Do not make promises you cannot deliver on. This will drive them bonkers. Always underpromise and overdeliver.

- The Sensitive Communication Style – This communication style tends to defer to others a lot. They seem open and polite on the outside, but their body language reveals otherwise. They may stir up trouble in the background if they do not agree with what you are saying even though they are saying they agree with you on the outside.

Types of phrases you may hear include: "Whatever you would like to do."; "Can't we all just get along?"; "I think it is a good idea but if someone doesn't agree do not be surprised." Their body language may include downcast eyes, hunched, and they nod their head a lot. Other people tend to overlook them and disrespect them and the sensitive communication type may struggle with low self-esteem. However, observe and make sure that they are not being manipulative behind the scenes by sharing misinformation or gossip, crying or forming a clique to get what they really want done.

- How to Best Communicate

    - Be prepared to answer questions about details with them. Practice being open and acknowledge what they've said throughout the conversation. This will build the trust and confidence that they have in you and they may open up more to you.

- Be relaxed with them. Ask them what they think about things. They may not tell the truth so watch their body language. Be enthusiastic about what they have to say.

- Have clear deadlines and objectives with them so they will understand what is going on. Always ask for their input. This will help them feel relaxed and at ease.

o What to Avoid When Communicating

- Do not try to rush them into making a decision. They may feel pressured and will not say what they really think.

- Be open to the idea that they may not like what you are saying. They may agree outwardly, but not really. They may not always voice their opinion out loud. If you hear from others that they are talking about you on their back, do not take it personally.

- Try to avoid conflict. They will not respond well. If you do have to offer negative feedback, try to make it as gentle as possible.

• The Socializer Communication Style – This communication style loves to be around people. They are extroverted and like to be the life of the party. Expect them to say things like, "I'm open to getting this done in the best way possible."; "I respect your ideas."; "Let me tell you what happened at this awesome party last night." They also practice non-verbal clues like moving their hands a lot, making eye contact, and lots of laughing and smiling. Others can view them as over-the-top or shirkers.

o How to Best Communicate

- Let your personality and sense of humor show. Ask about their personal lives. However, try not to get off topic. Hedge the questions by putting a time limit on the question. For instance, you can say, "Let's catch up for about 10 minutes before we dive into the meeting."

- Be open and engaged when you listen to them. If they get off topic, politely try to steer the conversation back to the topic. You can laugh at their jokes and listen to their stories.

- Listen to their ideas but be mindful that they can be overly optimistic and not always realistic. When you offer feedback, ask them to walk you through their thoughts process so you can understand better, but do not ask the question in a sarcastic way.

- Take notes so they can look at the notes later. Pictures are also good to use when speaking with them. This helps them to pick up on information quickly since you may have wasted a lot of time entertaining them.

- What to Avoid When Communicating

    - Do not be short or rude. This will look like you do not care about what they have to say and then they may shut down. If they don't trust you, they may not be willing to communicate with you.

    - Do not try to cut them off. Let them talk and smile along. Then bring up the topic at hand. Be gentle and strategic in the ways you bring them back to focus.

- The Analyzer Communication Style – This type of communicator likes to go into details around how everything works. They are meticulous about the details. They look at you in the eyes and say what they need to say without much embellishment. They are also neutral with their body language and appear comfortable and at ease. If they do not understand something, pay attention and see if they burrow their eyebrows or squints their eyes. Others see them as thinkers and sometimes people may get annoyed with them because of their focus on details.

    o How to Best Communicate

        - Be organized and be on time. They will do their part to be prepared to the best of their abilities and expect you to be prepared too.

        - Provide as many pertinent details up front and give them room to work independently. Charts and graphs are good. The more proof you can provide in the beginning, the easier the conversation will flow.

        - Be open to them double-checking your work. Do not take it personally, rather, value their attention to detail because it is a good character trait to have.

    o What to Avoid When Communicating

        - Do not use negative language when offering feedback. Try to be as positive as possible. Also, do not make personal attacks when providing feedback. Keep the feedback to the details only.

        - Try to keep the conversation on track. Do not ask questions about how they feel. Frame your questions to ask them what they think about the facts.

- They may not be as open to hearing about your personal life or small talk. So try to keep the anecdotes to yourself. However, the anecdote may just be what is needed to get them to open up. Keep the anecdote about children or pets and then see if they open up or not. If they do not open up, do not push it.

- Do not belittle them or talk condescendingly to them. Let them know that you value their work or insight and they will go above and beyond for you.

As you think about different communication styles, what is your style? What is your dominant communication style? What is your secondary communication style? Knowing what communication style you are helps you to understand the communications styles better and also helps you figure out how to explain to people the best way to communicate with you.

Most people have a combination of all communication styles so it is ideal to try and pick out the main communication type someone has and then apply the communication style strategies that are closely related to their most-dominant communication style. The more you practice communicating with the various styles, you will be able to be more nuanced in the way you communicate with people.

Another major component of having successful relationship management is conflict resolution. When dealing with relationships, conflict is bound to happen. Firstly, accept that conflict will happen. Conflict is nothing to be afraid of nor is conflict good or bad. Conflict is conflict. It is a human emotion that you will run into at some point in your life so it is good to know that it is going to happen and prepare yourself for when it happens. However, to successfully manage them you need to follow a few steps.

- Wait. When conflict first happens, you can pause for a moment. If you need to take a deep breath and count to ten, do so because it could save you from saying something that you regret. When you wait for a brief moment, it gives you time to collect your thoughts. Sometimes to resolve conflict, you can wait and agree to come back to the discussion once everyone has cooler heads.

- When it is time to resolve a conflict, first try to understand the reasoning behind the conflict. Great questions to ask include:

    o How can the conflict be resolved? - What would everyone deem as an acceptable response to solving the conflict? What are the tangibles and intangibles that can cause the issues to be resolved? Are you angry at a specific action or multiple actions? Knowing this can help you get to the root of the conflict.

    o What do you want out of conflict? - Knowing what you want to get out of the conflict resolution is important because it let you advocate for yourself and for your interest. What are non-negotiable for you when trying to resolve conflict? Also, what are you willing to compromise on? If you know this, this can help save time when in the middle of conflict resolution.

    o What triggered the anger? – What event caused the issue to boil over in the first place? Was it one event or a series of events? When you are discussing the conflict, are you discussing issues that occurred after the initial trigger of conflict or are you discussing what caused the conflict in the first place?

    o What interests do we both have that will see this resolved satisfactorily? – What are the common issues that both parties have interests in that can cause resolution? Are there things that you both can compromise on so the issue can be resolved quickly?

- Is your conflict a real issue or is your conflict an issue because you are a drama king or drama queen? – The answer to this question requires serious self-awareness. Sometimes we are being dramatic and our emotions cause us to blow things out of proportion. When trying to resolve conflict, make sure that the issue is not because you are upset. Make sure that it is because there is an actual issue at hand.

- Use neutral language. Try not to use language that uses blame language. Instead of saying words like "You did this" or "You did that", place the emphasis on how you felt as a result of the action. Take your time. Great advice is to use the 'Is it kind, it is true. Is it necessary' by Shirdi Sai Baba. If one of these is not met, do not say it. Only say words that meet all of these criteria.

- Do not offend people. Do not go low or make personal attacks. When people are talking, you can repeat what they are saying and try to use the words, 'I understand that you said...' or "I think I heard you say…" This helps the other party know that you are interested in what they are saying. This also slows down your angry response. That way the other party knows that you are listening.

- View the problem independently of the person. This is a wonderful piece of advice because it helps you remember that the other party is just a person. The behavior is what you have an issue with, not the person. This will definitely help you not say things that you wish you did not say.

- Maintain respect. Some relationships last a lifetime so you do not want to say something that will hinder the relationship down the road. When you say something, remember that you cannot take it back. Therefore, mind what you say because it could be the source of further conflict down the road.

- Try to understand first and then try to be understood. This helps you to let the other party feel understood, builds trust and lets them know you are trying to resolve the issue.

- Talk from a place of sadness, not anger. When speaking from a place of sadness, it allows you to be more vulnerable than when you are angry. It also opens up your senses to be nicer to someone else since you are in a vulnerable state.

- In the same vein, try to be open to other people's perceptions. Some people may perceive things differently than you and that's ok. Be open to listening to their perception and take responsibility for offending others even if you did something unintentionally.

- Take responsibility quickly if you are at fault. Take responsibility quickly sometimes if you are not at fault. Sometimes taking responsibility for issues that you may have not really helped resolve the issue. This is an act of good faith and helps mend conflicts faster than if no one wants to take responsibility. This also means taking responsibility for your feelings. Instead of saying what the other party did, explain the emotion that you are feeling. This put your feelings out in the open, clears your chest, and then opens the door to a faster resolution.

- Here's a handy formula to use when expressing your feelings in the middle of resolving conflict:
    - I feel (explain the emotion. If you can draw from your varied emotional library this is a good time to do so.)
    - When you (describe the behavior that made you feel the emotion objectively)
    - Because (what was the result of the behavior)
    - I would like (make a request of what the person can do to resolve the issue in the future. The other party may be open to doing this behavior and they may not be.)

- Go directly to the source of the conflict when trying to perform conflict management efficiently. Do not go to someone else about an issue you are having with someone else. This creates more layers that may have to be resolved later on down the road. When you feel an issue, go to the person who is the cause of the issue and let them know what the issue is. Then let them know you are serious about resolving the issue. After you reach some type of resolution, let the conflict be over. Avoid gossiping about the resolution to others.

- Listen. Be empathetic. Try not to take notes while listening to the other party. It can give off the vibe that you are not listening to what they have to say.

- Avoid trying to resolve conflicts by using written modes of communication like emails, texts, or letters. This helps because meanings can be lost in translation over the written word. However, if you must write to keep records of the meaning in a business setting, keep the correspondence professional because the written communication could be accessed by superiors in the future.

- Sometimes you can let your final demands that would resolve the conflict go. If you are unwilling to compromise your requests, the conflict may never be resolved. Be willing to compromise. This does not mean you are weak, it means that you have a solution that everyone is ok with and you become the hero.

- If you have to give feedback, frame it with the 'what-what-why' technique for giving feedback. First, explain what happened that causes the issue in the first place. Give examples. Then follow up with what should have happened to make the situation better. You can end the feedback with why this is a better reaction to the said issue and how it will prevent any conflict in the future.

- If you need a break in the middle of resolving a conflict, take it. Then come back to the discussion. You're human and the other person is human. Sometimes as you discuss the source of the conflict, emotions come rolling back and you or the other party gets upset again. Take the break, take a deep breath, and come back prepared to begin resolving the issue all the way over again.

- Practice. Keep practicing. Conflict resolution is not going to be solved overnight. If at the first time you are not perfect, do not panic. You will continue to improve. You will continue to know how to communicate with others with the communication style that's most effective for them to reach resolutions for conflict.

Communication skills, conflict resolution, and conflict management skills are at the heart of relationship management. These skills with be modified according to what type of relationship that you are trying to manage.

How to Manage Different Types of Relationships

How do you handle relationship management with various components of your family? This section gives you the best practices to use when managing the varying nature of relationships in your life.

Family

You can't choose your family but you can manage your relationship with them. Most people tend to want to have a close family unit, especially with their nuclear family. But in order to do so, you have to manage the relationship. Communication is key in helping you develop the relationship you want to with your nuclear or extended family. Families have so many layers so be careful with how you manage relationships because you cannot change your family. However, when dealing with family if the relationship is toxic, you can be open to cutting off the relationships if after talking, your family members do not want to acknowledge the conflict that you have with them. Do not be disappointed if your family does not always act the way you want them to act. They are human after all. However, here are some great tips to help with managing the relationship with your family.

- Communicate regularly. Be consistent in your communication schedule. With spouses and children, a consistent communication schedule helps them to see how important they are in your life and helps create small traditions among you that build the trust and love in the relationship.

- Consider initiating a regular family meeting for members or your nuclear family. This allows all grievances to be aired out and helps to build rapport amongst the family members.

- For your extended family, try to arrange a trip or time that you can get together outside of the holidays, so you are deepening the familial bond.

Friendships

Some friendships are those that you have to speak to the other person consistently in order to keep the friendship alive. Some other friendships are such that you can pick up right where you left off. You know the nature of your relationship and can adjust accordingly. With the advent of technology, it is easier to stay in touch with friends. Just like any relationship, create a regular communication schedule. With friends, pay attention to what they may not be saying. Be interested in their lives and pick up on any body language that may give their true feelings. Other tips include:

- Evaluate your friendships intermittently to make sure that the relationship is still working for both of you.

- Sometimes friendships change and are not the same. Children, spouse, and jobs can get in between friendships. Allow the friendship to develop organically and maintain the relationship according to changes in your lives.

Romantic Relationship

Relationships can fail when people who are in the relationships stop maintaining the relationship. With a romantic relationship, you have to continue to communicate and trust one another over the length of the relationship. Non-verbal clues are very important to observe in a romantic relationship especially the longer the relationship. When you hug and kiss your partner, how do they respond? When you want to talk and spend time together, how do they respond? Direct communication is also helpful. Check in every now and then and make sure everything is on the up and up.

- Keep things spicy. Do not be afraid to try things. Of course, try only what you and your partner are both comfortable with. It doesn't have to be just sexual things. You can change your routine to add some variety to your lives.

- Set aside time for you both. If you have children together, it is important to continue to bond without them so you can maintain your spark together.

- Resolve conflicts quickly. Conflict management is extremely important in relationships because sometimes conflict can bubble, fester, and damage the relationship beyond repair. The quicker you can resolve an issue, the better.

Coworker Relationship

There is a famous saying that states "Do not be friends with your co-workers." Keep the relationship professional. That's an interesting advice because the type of relationship you have with your co-workers depends on the culture of the office. Some workplace environments are really relaxed where co-worker relationships thrive. Other company atmospheres are cutthroat and competitive. Once you pick up on the company culture, you can decide how to move forward.

- Do not be the negative Nancy in the office. People do not like to be around negative people. Make sure that you are bringing positive energy to the workplace and not bogging it down with your drama.

- Be the co-worker others want to work with. If you are the type of co-worker that works and communicates well, others will want to be around you. This is important because if you ever move up in a company, your co-workers' opinions matter.

- Always respect people. You never know when they may be your boss. Do not let a nasty attitude come back to bite you in the butt.

Ultimately, the most important thing about relationship management, no matter what setting, is to always check in with your emotions. Being self-aware helps you have better relationships. Always check to see that you are being the best person that you can be in any relationship. If at any point, you realize that someone does not like you or you no longer want to continue in a relationship in the same capacity as before, it is your right to change your mind and adjust your behavior accordingly. Always be mindful that relationships can change and be okay with that change. As long as you are doing the best you can do in any relationship that is all that is required.

Other Tips for Managing Relationships

If you have the core skills of communication and conflict resolution, you will be able to successfully manage any type of relationship. Other great tips that you want to have when managing relationships include:

- Let other people know you are acknowledging their feelings. If they have strong feelings of anger or happiness, let them know that you understand their feelings, try to have empathy, but do not dismiss or belittle their emotions. A simple acknowledgment is great because it helps to build trust.

- If you ever get into an intense argument, focus on solutions instead of blaming people. It helps move the conversation forward. Anger is pointless. If at any point you get angry, acknowledge the anger then focus on a way to move forward.

- Be supportive. Always be supportive of people in whatever capacity possible. People never forget how you make them feel.

- Focus on yourself. Do not leave your support systems at the expense of maintaining a relationship. This is especially true in familial and romantic relationships. Do not feel the need to put all your needs aside because if at any point the relationship is lost, you will no longer know who you are.

- The most important thing to remember with relationship management is that you can never change the actions of people, but you can change how you react to them. This piece of advice will save you lots of heartbreak.

- Successful relationships take work. You will not always be compatible with people and they may not always be compatible with you. Everyone will not always like you and you may not like everyone else. That is ok. It is a part of life. Treat everyone the way you would like to be treated and the rest tends to work itself out.

In conclusion, emotional intelligence takes work but it is not impossible. For Valerie, she has learned how to develop her emotional intelligence from scratch and has learned quite a few tips along the way. For her, she noticed how much easier her life has become since she began to develop and embrace emotional intelligence. She is more in tune with herself and her feelings. She considers herself healthier in all aspects — emotionally, spiritually, and physically. She is more in tune with the feelings of others and is able to read what they are saying to her with their words and with their non-verbal clues. Her family life is thriving because she communicates how she feels. Valerie is also able to handle conflict easily without holding grudges or being bogged down in negativity. Her co-workers see how great a communicator she is and her bosses are looking forward to promoting her one day. She would not have been this way if she had not been forced to do so, but she is grateful for how emotional intelligence has improved her life exponentially.

Do not be like Valerie! Do not wait for the relationship to fail, for you to lose your health and mind, or for any other catastrophic incident to happen before you see the importance of being emotionally intelligent. You've made it to the end and the next step is in your hands.

Chapter Highlights

- Relationship management is all about how you handle the different relationships in your life. It is the last step in becoming emotionally aware.

- When you see the good as a core foundation of your relationship management skillset, you will always be able to effectively manage relationships.

- Always pay attention to people's non-verbal clues. It often states how they really feel. Practice adjusting your communication styles and conflict relationship skills to improve your relationship management.

Do the Work

Here are some great relationship scenarios for you to try out on your own. This helps you to think through ways to manage relationships and apply the concepts learned in this chapter. There is no right or wrong answer. You can take this practice to the next level by role-playing with friends.

1. Your significant other has been acting distant lately, but every time you ask them what is wrong, they say nothing is the matter. How should you proceed?

    A. You can take them for the word at it and do not push it. They'll tell you what is wrong eventually.

    B. You can dig deeper because you know that something bad is going on. They are probably cheating on you.

C. You can beg them to tell you what is wrong with them because you know something is not right.

D. You can take them at their word.

2. You were just upgraded to a manager position at your job. You have a co-worker who is having a difficult time in their personal life. Their hardships are causing you to pick up their workload and stay late at work. You want to be empathetic to their needs, but you do not want to stay late at work and do work that you are not getting paid to do. How should you react?

   A. You can talk to them to see what you can do to help that does not require you doing their work. Also, make them aware that they need to do their work or take a leave of absence because it is affecting the team negatively.

   B. You can talk to your boss to see if they can talk to them. That way you are not putting your friendship on the line.

   C. You can be nice to your friend and co-worker so you can maintain the personal relationship outside of work. The hardship should not last that much longer.

   D. You can rule with an iron fist. You are the boss and they need to learn how to handle their personal life and their professional life. You do not want other people on your team to think that you are showing favoritism.

3. Your family loves you and always wants to see that you're thriving. You casually mentioned that you received a salary raise with your new promotion. You have one family member, in particular, who asks you for money, but do not want to give them the money at all. What should you do?

   A. To test them and see if they really need the money or not, ask them why they are asking you for money. Then create a contract for them to sign before you loan them money.

Include the date that they will be paying you back and the repercussions if they do not in the contract.

    B. You just ignore their calls, texts, and emails. They'll be all right. You cannot be responsible for people outside of your nuclear family.

    C. You should get them the loan. If they do not pay you back, never give him another one.

    D. Communicate honestly with them. Let them know you feel uncomfortable with giving them a loan but you still love them. Then deny giving them the loan.

4. Your friendship with your very best friend has changed ever since they got married. They do not keep in touch like before and aren't acting like they were before the marriage. How should you handle the new dynamic in your friendship?

    A. You should realize that things have changed in your friendship and give your friend time to adjust. Everything will settle and go back to normal in the friendship soon enough.

    B. You need to call them and communicate how you feel. By doing this, you ensure that the relationship doesn't get out of hand.

    C. Ignore your friend the same way that they are ignoring you. True friends do not treat their friends like this too.

    D. You should end the friendship because they have outgrown the relationship and not being the friend that they need to be.

5. You feel a little out of whack and you are not sure who to talk to about all the feelings you have been experiencing. You discuss the changes with a friend in confidence but soon find out that this

friend has told everyone your personal business. How should you respond?

A. You should not do anything. If they are your friend, they are well within their rights to share your personal information with everyone in your friend group. All of your friends have the right to know.

B. You should confront them directly and let them know that they should never talk to you again. The friendship is over.

C. You should bring in all your friend and you all can talk about your issues together. But also let the friend know that you did not like their behavior.

D. Exclude yourself even more from the group. Everyone is going to think that you are weird anyway.

Conclusion

Thank you for making it through to the end of this book. Let's hope it was informative and able to provide you with all of the tools you need to achieve your ultimate goals whatever they may be.

In this book, you have learned what emotional intelligence is and the four components that make up emotional intelligence which are self-awareness, self-management, social awareness, and relationship management. Self-awareness is all about being in tune with your emotions and behaviors, while self-management is all about how you manage said emotions. Social awareness is how you can observe and pick up on the dynamics of social settings and relationship management are consists of identifying, analyzing, and managing the varying relationships in your life. Each component works together and can be improved. You can decide to tackle each component one by one so you do not feel overwhelmed when trying to improve your emotional intelligence. The journey to improving your emotional intelligence is a marathon, not a sprint. So there is no need to rush. Instead, commit to making steady baby steps.

The next step is to start to put what you have learned in this book to use. Do not delay. The longer you wait, the greater the wait to mastering emotional intelligence. Do not be surprised to see the amazing results that daily attention to improving your emotional intelligence will bring. You can re-visit any section of this book at any time in order to reference what was taught. Thank you for taking the time to read this book.

Thank you.

www.ingramcontent.com/pod-product-compliance
Lightning Source LLC
Chambersburg PA
CBHW021130080526
44587CB00012B/1223